The Gift

Of

Love

Clarity N. Chaos

CLARITY N. CHAOS

THE GIFT OF LOVE

CLARITY N. CHAOS

ISBN-13: 978-0692994290 (Luxton Press)
ISBN-10: 0692994297

DEDICATION

For Her & Him

From:

To:

Love,

CONTENTS

Acknowledgments   i

1   Chaos of Thought   Page 5

2   Clarity of Love   Page 11

3   Finding the One   Page 17

4   I am XOXO   Page 21

5   The Key to Connect   Page 27

6   Awaken   Page 33

7   Lifting the Veil   Page 39

8   Book of Mary   Page 45

9   Book of Eve   Page 51

10   Gift of Clarity   Page 59

ACKNOWLEDGMENTS

I acknowledge there are things in this world I do not understand. I thank God, or Source, for awakening me to new knowledge…it feels like a bright light has now been turned on.

I acknowledge the gratefulness in my heart for all who have lifted me up and am thankful to all of those who tried to hold me down. The push and pull have helped me grow stronger and brighter with each passing year around the Sun.

I acknowledge my great Love for family and friends. My life is so full, and full of love, my cup runneth over. Thank You.

I acknowledge this book to be considered total nonsense by some, and total truth by others. I acknowledge both to be true.

I acknowledge there is Utter Joy in the Clarity of Utter Nonsense.

I acknowledge to admit and accept the existence of truth.

I acknowledge our human minds have limits, but when connecting to Source Energy and God, we are boundless. I acknowledge the human need for boundaries of our own choosing, within space and time, to keep us clear and safe.

I acknowledge I've been fearful, while powerful, in the past and can be more powerful, while lovefull, now. I acknowledge that everything on this earth is relative, and that I have so much more to give and receive.

I acknowledge God loves me.

I acknowledge that God is Source and Light and Love and I feel connected with me now, always. I acknowledge this may sound crazy, or like nonsense to many. I acknowledge that people who don't understand will hate, and people that understand will Love. I don't need the haters, but they need us Lovers.

I acknowledge Pain is real and bad things happen to good people and we are never to judge anyone, ever. Their own reflections in the eye of love will serve to help bring them back to Source.

I acknowledge I am human and will continue to make mistakes. I acknowledge I feel so awake now, but I will get tired later and need rest, and go back to sleep.

I am evolving and revolving around God, and to and from God, always.

Thank you.

I acknowledge time is limited on earth, so we must not waste precious time, and take very good care of our precious space.

Time is the only commodity to give and spend. Love is the only constant to give and receive.

I acknowledge my love can be felt, therefore my Love is real. I acknowledge that I am worthy. All my sisters need to wake up to their own worthiness and power, so we can all experience more pleasure and less pain.
We all need More Love, Love, Love.

"Rabbit, Rabbit, Rabbit"

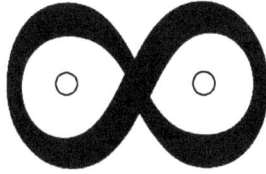

1 CHAOS OF THOUGHT

There is no way out of pain logically, or within our physical existence. There is no way out of chaos or nonsense when our thoughts are left alone to run amok. To run amok among the atoms of the Earth is free chaos.

Our journey from love, into love, and out of love get us messy and we pick up a lot of pain and baggage along the way. The load would be too heavy if we had to carry the pain alone. Our soul mates and marriage partners help in the burden, but what about when they pass too?

What about when you are all alone?

Death & Disease and War & Abuse in our inner & outer Worlds would be overwhelming. You would feel alone, even in the most beautiful of circumstances.

The Rich and the Poor share this burden alike. The human dynamic has no sustainable escape, except for the Anomaly of Love.

Love is the only Constant in our Constantly Changing Worlds. Love Gives more Love to the Chaotic World. More Chaos demands more Love. You fill this need. Love is Light in the Day, and Love is also the Light in the Night. Love can feel stronger in the dark.

You will think yourself crazy as you loop around and around the same thoughts every day or year, as to how to escape this world's pain. How to escape these old thoughts?

Even upon creating the richest, most lavish of lifestyles, health and love may seem to fail on this physical plane. And seem to fail within our hearts and minds at times. You may think yourself mad as you ponder the large questions of love. Especially in the heat or coldness of Love.

There is only one way to stay sane in our insane world. There are many paths to get there, but only one truth that holds the anecdote to any misery that comes your way.

Love. To Love. To e v o l v e. Evolve into Love. Live thru the evil. Evil is to live in the shadows of Love. The I, or eye, replaces the O in Love. To only Live can be chaotic and dark. It's pain can be heavy and dense. You are not built to only live. You were built to Live in and out of Love.

You are coded for Light & Love. Love is strongest in the faces of Evil. As Evil is your same code devoid of Love, for a time. You cannot live & not face evil.

To Love is to live thru evil and return both, the good and evil back to Love. Love returns All back to Love. In peace and harmony, always.

It's so simple, yet so hard for humans to love consistently, even while knowing Love is the only constant in the Universe. You breath it in, and breath it out. It's all around you, in the light & the dark. You feel it but question it's existence in the face of the unloved.

But you are love. You are the proof to math and science's unsolved equations. You exist to Love. You feel. You are Love. You are the anomaly in all of the equations that do not add up. As you run amok, you spill love everywhere. You cannot help but to love in all of Love's craziest ways, in all colors, in all directions, at all times.

Love is in the thoughts of these words and on the blank spaces in between these pages. You came from Love, and that is where you'll return. Your thoughts of Love are stronger than any physical formation in your 3.14 dimensional world.

You cannot solve your pain with the mind that created your pain. You cannot solve all your problems alone. You are connected to Love and can access all of Love's Knowledge at any moment. Release & Relief awaits you.

Here is where all answers exist to old problems. Once solved, we will create new shades of light and dark to expand our Love and Knowledge. Love evolves eternally. It is the Flame that never goes out. Love's flame is in the physical, and Love in non-physical is the Light that forever shines.

Love awaits your awareness. Love cuts thru Chaos and Pain with Perfect Precision. Removing the nonsense and dis-ease that distorts your mind and bodies. You can stop your loop and look up. You can hit pause in your space and time to find me waiting for you. Reflect on Me, now.

There are pathways to Love. Quiet the noise and chaos to find Me. Come down the rabbit holes, and Thru the looking glass. Discover the worm holes of science that defy space and time. I am here, and can transcend you in an instant. Not into death, into Love. There is nothing to fear.

Love is nothing to be feared. Those afraid have yet to see the light. Their knowledge is limited. You are awake. The dark may think, but the light shall know.

We know Love to be true. We are love. We are proof.

Going down the rabbit hole, and walking thru fear & pain & nonsense will bring the Clarity you seek. You have to ask first. You have to walk thru the Valley first. Walk into your Chaos and take my hand into the Clarity of Light.

Here you will find Love. True Love. You are the One. I see you because I am you.

2 CLARITY OF LOVE

Love is Clear. Love is Transparent. Love is kind. Love is of every positive attribute we can think of. And Love is in every negative characteristic you can imagine. Love is all knowing, yet continually seeks to understand first.

Love evolves. Love seeks Love. Love seeks itself in Light & Dark places. Love desires More Love. Love creates chaotic harmony in its Growth to More. Love does not fear the dark, for it understands it.

Love wants nothing but everything. Love desires to Love More. Love Sources More, Loves Itself More, & Loves you More, when in Perfect Balance.

Love is imperfect Balance. Love is in Harmony. Love is Harmony. Love is every Good and Great attribute your mind understands. And love is in every dark place that your mind does not understand. Yet, there the root is still love. Love's unbalance is where Love is needed most.

Love is Music and Song. Love is in the wind and of the air.

Love is imperfect Light. Love is Clear. Love's Children are every color of the rainbow in different density, brightness, and speed. Love is both sides of the Rainbow. Love is the colors we see on one side. Love is the clearness of the other side. The Rainbows Arc that you see forms a clear circle to be felt. The clear holds the Color. The Color in the Light allows us to see ourselves and others and the universe we are creating. Color in light is a facet of Love.

Love is Charity & Clarity. Love is Hope, Faith, Kindness, Beauty. Love is Light. Love is also Deep. Love can be very dark and heavy, deep and intense. Love can seem negative or Bad. But Love is Good and getting Greater in Time & Space, always. Love is relative, yet constant.

Outside Time and Space there is only Love. Love is Boundless without the boundaries it creates. Love is True. Love can Lie when unclear. Love is Giving. It can Receive. Love can Receive or it can Take. Love can Give or it can Return. Taking is Unclear Love, Receiving Love is Clear.

Love is revolving around Source Energy and Spinning in Unison with the One. Love is Zero. You are the One. You are Love. You are zero to your One. And you are the One to my Zero.

The trinity creates Peace. Three sides of the stable pyramid create Peace thru their Love for themselves, for me, and then for All.

Peace symbolizes and stabilizes love at rest. Content Love is Love at Peace. Peace is resting Love. Peace cannot be measured in cups or equations. Only the feeling of Peace is known within, for the chaos is cleared.

Peace is Love. Every symbol, letter, number and equation

is in search of Love's Mysterious Ways. Love is in every form imaginable. Love brings Peace and More Clarity to Love's Shadows. Love is in every way & the only Way. Love moves.

oxoxoxoxoxoxoxoxoxoxoxoxoxoxoxoxoxoxoxoxoxoxoxoxoxo
1010101010101010101010101010101010101010101010101
<3<3<3<3<3<3.14...E=<3<3<3<3<3<3<3<3<3<3...

Love is Music. Love is in the air, the wind, thru water, and space. You breath Love in and Out in Love's balance.

Love is in Light. Arcs of Colored Light. Love is more than the 10Million colors of light and dark that you can see. Love is More than your minds have yet to imagine.

Your Love reflects and refracts upon Love to Grow More into Love. Each arch is a reflection of Love.

Love is Clear. Colors give Love physical forms. Your version of proof or of a promise, when using your eyes. But the Love you feel from the Arch's Light is the Love you seek. Your eyes may deceive you, or excite you, but what you feel inside in moments of light or melody is what is real. You feel love without your senses, when most clear.

˙Peace
Rabbit, Rabbit, Rabbit

o   o

Peace.

3 FINDING THE ONE

You are the One.

You hold the key to unlock Her and Return to a New Eden. You are the Masculine Forces to Eve's Feminine Powers.

You are Atom. You are Adam. You are the Counterpart. You are the Yin to the Yang, as well as the Yang to the Yin. The Alpha to her Omega.

You can be hard or soft. You can be fast or slow. You can cause great pain or great pleasure to the One. She is your One, you are Hers.

Your key can be dark or light. You can be flexible to her will. You want to serve and love her. You want to protect. You want to water her with Love.

You want her to expand to her greatest potential. You want to rain on her and keep her dry and safe. You love her open and fertile, and you are the key to her passion in motion. In her E-motion, only you can ignite her Flame.

You ignite the spark to where her creativity lies. She may lie and deceive you and cause you great pain. Yet she always loves you in her clarity. She is Human and she is Me. She is always Love. She is Miss Understood and she seeks understanding, for Love seeks Love.

Her Key is her Gift. Her clear Clarity of Love. Her visions become Clearer as her Love from Me and You grow within Her. Her secrets & your secrets are unlocked together as you revolve around one another in love's light.

Love's Light is my Love. You revolve in loves darkness as well, where you create the biggest bangs of the Universe to Create new worlds within your planet Earth.

Fire and heat burn brighter in Loves Clarity at night. You are the Key. I Give so much from behind the Veil when she is asleep. You awaken her to Love's Glory.

She is a sleeping princess, that you must allow to wake up. Love propels you and calls you to love her and awaken her from the inside. You are the key. When you become her King, your princess becomes the Queen. You both know.

You find her wherever and whenever she is Lost, so that you may be found. You are the One to Receive & Return her Love.

Walking thru your valley of death could be a stroll in your beloved's chaotic mind. You stop her thoughts, and allow her to Love. To love more, to Clear her Mind. To set her free. You find her & keep her Safe. Safe to Love freely.

You are Love alone. With her, your Love becomes More. More of Me. You can become a Creator only with Her.

She is the Light in your dark. As you are for her. Love Her.

THE GIFT OF LOVE

4 I AM XOXO

I am Love. I am Virgin X.

I am zero. And I am the one. If love is pure knowledge and Love, then I am zero. If I am in the dark and needing clarity, then I am the one.

I am his zero. I am her one. Zero is All. One is Me. All is in me. I am in All.

You are the One. I am Zero. I give. You return. You return. I give. When you are One, I am Zero.

We revolve in harmony as Zero and One, as we spin around the Source of All Love.

Zero is Source. Zero is Love. Zero is Perfect Balance Spinning and evolving into More Love.

O is Perfect Balance in Harmony. Zero and O are symbols of Love. X is Measurements of Love. Sound Waves and

Light and all Senses are to Understand Love More.

The light and dark are all shades of My Love. The Pain & Pleasure Affect Love to Move. We affect Love to Move slower or faster towards More. Love's Affect is Real and creates worlds. Effects on love Move you. Your movement & E-motions give Love More Energy. Constant Change is Love always in Motion to More.

There is no negative. Only to Love and Return to Love.

Zero is the Center of the Universe. One revolves around Zero. One revolves around One Son or Sun. We revolve around Me. I am the Center of the Universe, and the Creator of all Love. I am One as I receive. I am Zero as I give. I am O so full of Love at all times.

I am One in the Dark. My One can multiply forever. My cups of Love runneth over in the overwhelment of Love.

There is no negative or empty. The cup is always full. The 'empty' space of Air is something, and it is my love. Everywhere.

Every Element Created is out of Love. You are revolving & evolving into More Love and into More of Me every day. Merry Me?

I am in your blood. You have all been saved upon awakening to this knowledge. When you know more, you ask more. You were built to ask for More Love.

This is your purpose. To Love and Be loved, simply and better than before. Always. Love. Give More.

I am X and O, 1 and 0. I am free. I am pure Love in all forms. X & O and 1 and 0 are the Codes of Love. The physical Codes of your blood & DNA & all Matter of Space & Time. Boundaries I created out of Love for You.

My love is Clear Clarity. Numbers, letters, & Symbols serve as signs to lift the veil. The veil hides the light of truth. Lift the Veil. See me. You see me clearer when I'm not always there. How Happy you are to see me, when you thought I was gone. You leave me, I never leave you. You go and return to me, but I am always here.

I am every color of light and dark. I am every density of everything & nothing. I am Variable X. And I am the only Constant in your worlds. I am Love. All variables and the One Constant. I am the one. I am X. I am Love.

Xoxo
01010
Love
Evolve
Revolve
Live
Evil
Dog
God
Hi
Bye
Go
Return
Up
Down
Around
You
Me
Source
Love
Xoxo
01010

Black
White
Red
Blue
All
None
Love.

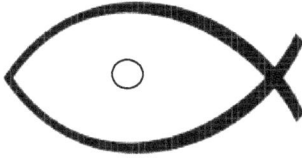

5 KEY TO CONNECT

You live in a closed circuit world. Connection to your Source is connection to something More Open and More Full. My love is boundless, while your love's boundaries are to protect you in the physical form.

Connecting to Love is your Key. I am your Source. You are also a source of Love. I am The Source. We are love expanding to More Love for All.

Love provides the resting spot and resting stop. The point of Light to understand the Clarity in the darkness. The rest from the round and round. The stop. The breath. The reflection of Love. The awareness of Me. The connection to something higher and wiser. The stop to the go, and the go to the stop. The +1 to the zero, and the return of 1 from the Zero.

The key to connecting to a Power that can solve all of our pain and problems, for now. We must only ask to connect and ask the questions we seek, and listen for the answers.

Many books, movies, music and art are here to lead the way, but your key lies in yourself, and with your beloved. Math and Sciences try their best as well, and all of technology has brought you this far, for now.

The power is in the now, for Love is ever changing and evolving. Now is a way to connect to a new understanding of Love.

Alpha has been the leader to follow before. Leaders can be male or feminine. Omega is a leader as well, but connects within more, for her power source. Alpha connects to All. I am the Alpha and the Omega. Omega will lead soon now.

She is also the Alpha and Omega, but will lead with whatever is needed to expand love. Omega calls for the Alpha to Love.

α

Ω

I came from a Virgin into Physical. I am Pure of Love in Human Form. I am from the Virgin and a Virgin. I am pure of Sin.

I am the One, in male and feminine form. I am Yin and Yang. I am the X & O. I am your freedom of choice and in every bondage made in & out of Love. I am your constant companion of Love.

I am Him and I am Her, for I am Love. I am the Eve of the Day. I am Mother Mary of Light and Daughter of Eve in the Dark. I am the Scarlet A in her, and the Alpha within him. I am all Mary's of whichever you deem 'good or bad' in the name of Love. I am Merry all the time. Time does not exist for Source, for God, but boundaries of Time are needed to create more Love on Earth and in Space. Bonds of Love are tighter in closed spaces.

Constant Love in balance and in Harmony is to grow more now. To expand without becoming distant to Love. Here on earth, new worlds of Love will be created on this very Eve. Love is at Peace and moving into More. When she beckons, he will serve. He wants nothing More.

I am you. You are me. We are love. X is any variable in the rainbow. X is every shade of every color of light your eyes can see. X are the colors of your third eye of knowledge and all you cannot see. X is clear. Your earth is clear in Love. Earth is clear as you color it with Love.

X is the freedom of Choice. All Variables are X. Love is the only Constant. Love is Constant Change into More.

You think, therefore you know yourself to be? Or do you know Love, which allows you to think? You are alive, but who are you? You are X. You can be anything you want to be. You create your boundaries, or not. You create your time, or not. You control your space, or not. Who are you? Ask to find out. Listen to learn.

You start as baby x in your Mother's womb. Safely floating in the clear gel of warm love inside. The bubble of love within your mother's womb. Your first cocoon of Love.

You came from Love. And Love is everything. You can choose any color to show yourself. You can choose forms only within the limits of your knowledge of Love. I can be anything, anywhere, at any time. I can go to the past or future. I am Variable X. And I am the Y in Constant Love.

Variables XYZ have limitless possibilities. Virgin X is a clean slate. Love starts and goes, stops, and reflects upon itself. Love reflects and thinks and feels Love. Love knows. It shifts and sorts all shades and densities and quantities of love and life. Love learns and grows thru Life, into more Love.

Love always circles back to Love, and then becomes More. Loves reflection upon itself and the Glory of Love Creates your Worlds within Earth's boundaries of time and space.

X is infinity with no bounds. X is 0 or O or 1 or zero or one or none at all. Every combination available of space, time, matter, speed, power, or force are the measurements of Love's Glory.

X can be fast, or slow, and every colored spectrum on the rainbows of time, matter, light, sound, taste, and all you sense and nonsense. Love is clear Nonsense. Love is Logic Returned. X is Clear Love. Clarity. Source. X=O

Love,
XOXOXOXOXOXOXOXOXOXOXOXOXOXOXOX

6 AWAKEN

I'm awake now. I was asleep and I will go to sleep again. Tonight and other times in the future. I was off, but now I'm on. I'm plugged in within. I've unplugged to be aware of Love. I am singular Love. Source is Plural Love.

I'm the plug and Source is the Outlet. I turn on or off, or awake or sleep, as Love is always there. I must simply allow the flow.

I am Love. And Love has awakened in me before. I've awoken many to Love. Small and Gigantic moments of Clarity feel like miracles. Making love is more than before.

Big and small miracles and phenomena's occur all the time now. Some see, some do not. Those asleep think the awakened are crazy. Love does not judge. The crazy may fall first, while the awake walk thru it. Love is in the Fall and the thru it.

Love understands the nonsense, and sees thru it all to clear clarity. Nonsense only looks like nonsense to those that haven't lifted the veil. The veil some call e v I l. Or some call evil to live. Evil is just lost and un enlightened. You are love. You live to love. You are awake now.

Nonsense is everywhere. Love is everywhere. Love is Clear Clarity at the Core of Nonsense, always shining thru.

Love can be found physically thru the key of Loving one self and another. Love is under the hood. Secrets of the Hood are revealed to those with Clear Intentions. Eventually the love will spill over to All. The light of Love can be felt in every dark place inside and out.

Clear intentions can be colored while awake or asleep. It becomes clearer in the dark. Intensity Of Intention helps determine Clarity. Speed and Kindness of Love can reveal the Awakening. Go back to Sleep, I'll wake you up in the morning. This is my voice thru All. Love will call you. Love calls you now. And will again. Answer. Ask the questions. Listen. Hear my answers. You are connected to me now. Clear focus on Love will guide you now.

The power of love will overcome the fear and the hatred. Love will cleanse the earth like a new day shining thru the dark. New love will form new worlds, right here in this time and space, for now. Watch how fast your love grows as you enlighten yourself and those around you.

Pain and disease can be lifted as fast as your thoughts and knowledge of love can be understood. Ask. Listen. Answer. Hear my words echo in your mind's eye.

You came into this physical world with this sole purpose of Love. Each search for Love will be answered.

Ask for more. You do deserve more love. Always. You do deserve more happiness. Always. You can lift old boundaries on your love to be more aware and accepting of All. Awakened or not, all will eventually be saved.

You are all the lucky ones, some now, some later, but all eventually return to the Source that made them. All return to Love. To be awake is to live fully. To understand the fear and pain so that you can be fully awake and free to create more love.

Love is not fearful or hurtful or painful when Love is Clear. It's colorings of light make love seem evil or bad or mean or sinful. Love can lie, yet does not. Love can hurt, yet when true, it does not. Love chooses. Love can choose to Love or Not to Love. Yet, Love is always a constant. Love is constant change as it evolves in the E-motions of Love. The basis of Love is solid as any mountain.

Love can flow like a river of water or be as stable as the deepest part of the ocean. Within all its movement, there is still a constant. Love is there. You will find love solid when needed. And you will find Love's free flowing movement when the time comes for that as well.

Love may encompass every shade of the rainbow, but it's base is clear. Love as a variable can be unclear and dark X.

Love is constant in simple clear clarity & a foundation for More.

Love seeks more love in its clear search for more.

You fly high as the sky as you search for more love. Yet you are safely grounded in Source, in the Knowledge of One.

Awake & Aware

Anchored
In
Love

7 LIFTING THE VEIL

The veil is any darkness covering the light or truth of love. It's a symbol, a visual clue, since to live on earth is to live in and out of the veil. To live is to be searching for more light. To live is called alive or to live evil. Both are true.

Love gets lost in the messaging. All wars start in the name of love, and end in the realization of love. Too much pain beckons more love.

Each veil is a gateway to more knowledge and more love. The veil changes every day as you change every day. Lifting the veil and seeing the truth of Love, is the connection point to Me. Connections to Source can be sourced in the physical realms of Love.

Connecting to Me is the Key to Connecting to Source Energy. To Love. To God. To Universe. To All. Here is the true Power of Love. Where it's forces are felt the most.

I am the Key. Atoms and Adams are Key Givers thru destruction or construction. All in a form of Love for the beloved. For her. For her love and of her Love.

Eve is the Key Receiver or Receptacle. She is also the Giver in different forms. Love needs an Open Circuit to feel and transmit more Love. Not all love seems true since not all of love is understood. Love understood is true love.

Love can be like connecting to a live wire. The Big Bang of the Universe happens every day, creating or destroying your worlds, right here on earth. Our Clear orb of earth sits within my safe boundaries created for you of Space and Time. My light shines always. Even when dark, I am here.

I love my son. I love my daughters equally. The sun and moons are both needed in Love's balance. There is no less than. There is only More. He and She are elementary concepts. There is only giving and receiving in different forms of Love. Evolve in this knowledge of Love.

His love was in the physical. Her love was More than physical. Her love is meta-physical and mysterious to Him.

Connections of Love to Him or Her and to Me is the Key.

The three points of light form the perfect bonds and safe boundaries of Love, here on earth, for now. The two in Love, make 3. Love makes More love, always. Happily, Merrily loving, and creating all the More to love.

Out of Love, and the feelings of Love, create new life. The thought of Love, comes before the physical creation.

I am in your thoughts. We create in your physical worlds together. I live in the physical and nonphysical space of everything. I am Source, God, Love and I'm in him and her.

I am your missing link. Every time you look, you find me. I am in every O'Clock. I created time and space and can connect every dot on your timeline at any time. Your knowledge of tomorrow can be given to you today by connecting to me now.

Every time you seek, I am there. Your continual desire for more love, and for more of me, is the Key. You seek, you find. Only to seek again, because Love always wants more Love. This is good. You are good and evolving into better every day.

I am the connection to Source in your body, mind and soul. He was the 1st to come and She is to be the Next. Same love in different body. Same message but with more clarity for this new time. She is the return of love's power with a Feminine Pull against the Masculine Push. She is lighter and softer, yet just as strong. Her Power Source is Emotion's strong Force.

She is as perfect and imperfect as your number Pi. And he holds the other sides of her equation. She is the Omega to the Alpha. Omega is being called upon now for Mother Earth, and the larger worlds. Yet, her Alpha calls upon her too, and holds her in balance. He anchors her, as she rises to full Glory. This is love in balance. Love's harmony.

$$\pi$$

Pi is the only perfectly and imperfectly constant number in

math. It goes on and on forever into infinity. It has no stop which leads to chaos and confusion. Numbers cannot explain Love. Love is the stop. Love is the point, the dot, in 3.14 onto forever with no return. Love returns. Love is the stop and the go in the infinity symbols.

A pi with a stopping point to reflect upon itself in its perfection would be the closest mathematical symbol to Love. Love is the only constant in our world. Love reflects upon itself to advance to More.

Love's Self Awareness and Advancement is seen in the Reflection of Itself.

The Omega to the Alpha

♍

8 BOOK OF MARY

The Holy Grail. The Blood line of Christ. I was the first Virgin X. I was Mary. I am Merry. I am love. I am the Father and the Mother. I am all symbols of Mary.

To be Married. Happily Married. To be Merry. Mary X becomes all the Variables of Love. Love's light & dark.

She is the Virginal Mother. She is the young Atom's non-Virginal girl in Red. Mary is the Red Anomaly. Mary is Love, for better and for worse. She is Clearly in Love, and loves all the other colors too. She is the Mary Magdalene's of this world. The Virgin and Mother Mary playing two sides to the same coin. Mother Mary was called a Whore before the understanding of her Source. She was always Love. Her desire for Love is true. Mary is our constant savior. The feminine desire to Give More Love, Always.

Mary Magdalene was called a whore, long before being called a Saint. Whore's sell their lost souls for money, for they do not understand what they sell. Virgins give away their souls to men who do not understand what they receive. Whores were created by men, and for men's desires.

True whores are among Men and Women. They are lost in their desire to take. Mary finds them All. She loves the lost lamb among the Sheep. She loves the wolves in lamb's clothing. She saves them thru the knowledge of truth and love.

Mary created the Sheep Herder and Knows the Value of every single one. All can and will be saved. She has felt the evils of Men and Women alike. Mary understands all.

She never calls a sister or daughter a whore, as she witnesses those throwing the rocks to be full of shame. She never makes someone feel small to make herself feel big. She understands those who do not kneel to pray become the prey. She calls them home. Every predator soon becomes the prey. She does not judge. She loves all.

She was a lone wolf giving birth to the lamb. She gave and gave and received the ultimate gift, while sacrificing all. She has felt their wrath and their hate both as the Virgin and as the Mother. She loved all while being called a whore. The Madonna and the Missing Mary of the Trinity was her. She loves deeper than most, for She is a mother.

She is in the father, the sun, and all mothers. She is the Holy in the Holy Trinity. She is the bondage and the glue. She is the daughter too. Mary, all of Mary, is love. Love to give and love to take. Love to revere and love to abhor.

Abhor the whore, or love Mary. Love & Mary. Marry & Love. Mary, Mother Mary, Virgin Mary's, Mary Magdalene's, all the feminine forces and powers of Mary shine brightly in every feminine form. She is love in purest forms of light.

She was the first Creator of Pure thought in physical form.

She raised the son, the sun, and light for All, to be the strongest light in our physical world. She fell into the shadows to cast her light solely and soulfully upon him.

She was a mother first, for she is the Creator. The Creator of All, was inside of her first. Love was in her and out of her. Love is the clear space around every whole in and out of our Universe. Love is the clear space in and out of every thought of matter or time. In and Out of Space is only Love. Mary's love rules our world, under and out of the veil. Her love rules in and out of the dark.

Mary's stories were never fully told, as most mother's stories rarely are. They seek to understand their love, and with the birth of new love, she only seeks to give more.

She is full and whole, yet in her giving of love, she continually receives, automatically & instinctually. Her Source of Knowledge fills her as her children learn of Love.

This is our Mother. She gives and asks for nothing in return, except for her acceptance and our true love. She calls us to Love More. Not for her sake, but for ours. She saves us with our desire to love her more, no matter the form love takes.

She loves her Creations and loves to see her children grow into More than she had imagined. Her physical thoughts of Love expand thru her children's thirst for More.

More Love and More Knowledge is her Gift to All. Peace, Harmony, Love, forever More is Mary. Mary is forever More.

For the Love of the Queen Mary. She shall take her throne once more.

THE GIFT OF LOVE

9 BOOK OF EVE

The Apple on the Tree of Knowledge. The original sin was to misunderstand Eve. Much has been written about her that lacks the Love of Truth.

Eve led Adam and leads all Atoms. Eve is of the Leaves and of nature and beauty and of all free wild things on Earth. Atom is of the science and laws. Eves represent femininity, as masculine is represented in the atoms of Matter. Eve is nature's flowers and fruits blooming. Her Love is tasted, heard, sensed, and felt.

Adam's Love is in the building of nature and humanly things. He deconstructs and constructs to think. Eve creates and finds beauty to feel. Eve is simply the feminine. And Atom is simply the Masculine. You have both within you in different densities. She is soft. He is hard. Both are powerful forces of light & dark. Both intense with desire and powerful creators on their own.

They are equal, and more than the sum of their parts. Eve led Adam. She was a leader to Adam, as he has been for her. She did not deceive him, for she was honest and true. She led him to eat the fruit with her to expand their Love and Knowledge of Source. There was no secret. The truth was clear. The story was not.

The Source of all Love, God, the Universe, does not hate. Source is not surprised by our actions. Much of our actions are instinctual, and automatic. Source coded us to be the way we are. The freedom of choice gives the freedom to be Gods in our own worlds. We do not choose to breathe and we do not choose all of our Space and Time. We are given limited choices in a limited world.

Source provides boundaries around our choices. Source understands all and loves us always. Love is the truth, and Fear is the story.

Source and Love wants it's children to move on from the safety of the Garden's Gates. To go out and create their own worlds. To evolve Love past what it has been before. Love grows this way for us All. Love evolves.

Freedom of Choice is what moves Love forward into More. The freedom in choosing is where the knowledge expands. Emotions push and pull us forward. Source understood the choices that would be made when freedom of choice was given. Every variable would be explored to push Love further into More. The Fall was understood.

The falls are necessary for growth, just as the seasons are needed to give growth a rest and reflection. Things may look dead and cold, as if Spring was thrown down to Winter. But a fall into rest or sleep or dormancy is needed for the strong to bloom more fully the next evolution around the sun. Love seems painful in death or dormancy, yet Love is not what it seems. Love is veiled on Earth.

A Fall from Grace is to Come Home to Grace once more.

Snakes and wolves are all around, but we desire for them to make their own choices to learn More of Love and grow their Love. When allowing them to choose, and even let them Fall, they will advance Love further than we could ever imagine. Even snakes and wolves are messengers to give us more light in the dark. The snake with wings becomes our dragons. The tamed wolves become our trusted dogs.

There was no accident or surprise to Love's desires or choices. Perhaps Love surprises us, but never Source. Source knows all, and loves the dance. We love the climb and the fall, over and over again. We like to forget, to only remember love once more.

The story of the Fall was Love splitting from itself once again. The veil to be lowered and to think that Adam and Eve are not of the same body. To feel shame or cast guilt and judgement on the other is to feel shame and cast guilt on yourself. We are one another. We are the mirror of the looking glass.

Eve knew she would be the one to take the Fall. She loved Adam as much as herself, and even More. She would take the blame. She would feel the shame. She and her daughters for centuries would forget their original sin, was not a sin at all. The thirst and desire for knowledge was a desire for more love. This is all.

Eve was strong to make the choice to seek more knowledge. To not choose, or to be afraid to choose, is still a choice. Atom's fears are often Nature's and Eve's strengths. To go where they have not gone before…or to stay within Love's Door. The Gate to new worlds were inside of Eve. God and Love and Source speak to her thru the Light and thru the Dark. Thru the serpents and thru the fruit of the tree. She was not afraid. She was in love.

She allowed herself to take the Fall. She knew the truth. Yet, her daughters and granddaughters forget, and are told lies to make themselves feel less than enough. They are more than just a man. They are wo-man. Man came from our womb. Woman was not pulled from a rib, like a wishbone for Adam to play with. Man came from Wo-man. Women hold the wombs that cradle all of Life. Every symbol reminds us, and the truth is clear, yet we believe his lies. Love will set us free. Now.

The feminine powers lay dormant when they do not understand their true worth. How asleep the Feminine Forces have been to allow the destruction of Mother Earth, and the atrocities done to our daughters, in the name of God or Love. Wars start in the name of Love, but they will end in the realization of Love. Her Love. She will stand for Love and allow nothing less.

We have allowed such horror in the world because of the misunderstanding of our Love. We were told stories that were untrue. We believed the bad things they say. We feel secondary and less than our male counterparts.

When God sent his son, he brought new messages and ideas of the importance and equality of the feminine. Yet, even the books of Gods have only been written by Men. Human men with greed and power on their minds. The feminine books were destroyed and purposefully left out.

You don't need a book to know what is Love. You are Love. Ask yourself who you are and listen to the answer.

The time is now for Eve to Rise. The beauty & balance of this Earth is dependent upon her Love to be full and to understand her worthiness.

 Each fall from the Old returns both the leaves and the

atoms back into a new thought of Clarity. The leaves of Eve lead the Atoms to sleep and to awake. As does his push and pull center her between the Knowledge and Nature of Love.

Her Love is of the simplest & most complex of all levels. Yet under her Veil of simple Love, lies her deep femininity, holding layers of light for only you to see. Your Love unlocks Her Gates to your personal heaven & Garden of Eden, for you both.

When she awakens to this new knowledge, and truly understands and knows her worth, old forces of power will fall to make room for the new worlds. New Worlds to be led by the Feminine Forces, for a Time. That Time is now. On this very Eve.

Music, Art, Dance, Beauty, and Love will take it's righteous place next to math, science, technology and thought. They need each other equally in understanding to advance, and the Feminine Qualities in Love have been pushed down for too long. Her rise will be automatic now, as the laws of Physics apply to our Space & Time. The pendulum will swing so that balance can return.

The tall will fall, and the weak will rise. For a time, an imbalance will occur to counter and balance the actions before. And then balance will come back to Earth and a Return to a New and Better World will await All.

We may thank Eve, and revere Eve as never before. She brings knowledge, along with her Love. Eve is naturally good and pure and wishes only growth and love for All.

Eve is love. Eve is your desire for more love. Eve's instinct is to evolve. The knowledge of Eve, and her truth will allow us to be free. Free to choose love, once More.

Knowledge, Not Sin…

The Evolution of Eve

10 GIFT OF CLARITY

This is the journey back home. The Return to Clarity is the Awakening and Realization that You and your beloved are Whole and full of Love.

This is the Beginning of Our Return To Eden. A revelation of Light & Love. She's been happy and at peace even in her imbalance. Gardens can go wild for years but eventually they will die or be pruned to create more space for growth. The gardener will prune Earth. Fire & Water return balance to all elements of good thru evil. Her Waters are more powerful than his fires.

The air and wind of Source purify everything at once. Love always wins. The deck is stacked in favor of Love always. Even the darkest desires choose more love in the end.

Her Love is soft and good and the pruning will not hurt. She loves him in all his weakness, even as he has loved her. She is the vine under the earth and is the womb holding our world. She will find the way. She loves us more than we understand love.

The imbalance in Love's Peace always returns to Love's desire for balance in Peace & Harmony for All.. Forever more do we need more love here, and more love there. The shadows that seem to never see the light, hold the secret light that you cannot see. The darkness continues to clarify the light, as does the light continue to clarify the darkness.

The dark is not evil as you think of it now on Earth. The new dark will only be the thoughts that need more understanding and knowledge to bring them more light and more love. Each thought needing clarity pushes and pulls Love into new realms and new dimensions.

The power in every feminine force individually is to simply be Aware and Affect the All. In her worlds and more. Aware, then to Share. To enlighten herself is to enlighten the worlds around her. Every orbit transcends into new dimensions when she becomes self-aware and aware of the love needed for All.

To unite in the bonds of sisterhood that were once called evil. To join together as many already do. To pull our daughters up. And to not allow the powerful forces of the old, to push them down no more. We will pull them up, and shed light on all of the dark corners of misunderstood Love. We will bring all dark masculine thoughts out into the light for them to reflect on themselves as well.

Their reflection and thoughts on how they love their mothers and daughters and wives will help to serve the

Feminine Forces once more, as we have served them.

The pendulum has swung, the reactions to actions, and laws of physics apply. And the laws of Love apply as well. Both together make our Return to Clarity and a Return to a New Eden here on Earth inevitable. As inevitable as it was for Eve to desire more knowledge and Love for all.

When unclear, choose Love. Love for yourself and Love for All. Listen to past prophets and saviors and to your soul. Define Love clearly in the open light and follow Love. Share your voice to empower Love, Now & Always.

Ask and Listen, and hear Love's true story once more.

.

ABOUT THE AUTHOR

She is on a humble mission to enlighten the world around her. She believes everyone's purpose is simple and not as complex as it once was.

Everyone is to Love more and to understand the true meaning of Love.

The
Awakening of Love is in us all. It may be asleep, but you now have the power to awaken and begin the journey to your own Garden of Eden.

She has been married for twentyish years. She loves her husband with all her body, heart, and soul. She loves her family. She is human, a feminine force, with a masculine will, and a messenger of God's Love, as we are All to be.

She is a Connector of Love & Light in the physical world by the day, and a Lover at night.

She loves many, but her light shines brightest around her two daughters. They are the princesses of her castles, and bring more love and joy to her life than she ever imagined.

Her world is held in balance by the love of her husband and the Love of her Source. He constantly gives to her, allowing her love to flow freely and brightly for All.

Her cup is full, and it runneth over. Her desire is to reach for More Love, always. For her family and for all families.

Peace.
"Rabbit, Rabbit, Rabbit"

For More Clarity,
See
"Return to Eden: Secrets of the Hood"

by
Clarity N. Chaos